8273
Race Cars

Race
Cars

by Sallie Stephenson

42585

Capstone Press

P.O. Box 669, Mankato, MN, U.S.A. 56002-0669

CIP
LIBRARY OF CONGRESS CATALOGING IN PUBLICATION DATA

Stephenson, Sallie.
Race cars / Sallie Stephenson.
p. cm. – (Cruisin')
Summary: Describes different types of race cars, outlines the safety features that make racing less dangerous, and takes a behind-the-scenes look at such racing events as the Indy 500 and Le Mans.

ISBN 1-56065-068-0:
1. Automobile racing – Juvenile literature. 2. Automobile racing-history – Juvenile literature. 3. Automobile racing – Dictionaries, Juvenile.
[1. Automobile racing. 2. Automobiles, Racing.] I. Title. II. Series.
GV1029.S767   1989
796.7'2 – dc20   89-77248
                                                                  CIP
                                                                  AC

PHOTO CREDITS

Compliments Valvoline, Inc.: Pages 4, 6, 10, 11, 12, 14, 15, 16, 18, 22, 23, 24, 25, 28, 29, 30, 31, 32, 33, 35, 37, 39, 40, 41, 42, 43, 44, 45, 46, 48

Compliments Newman Haas Racing: Pages 19, 20, 26

CAPSTONE PRESS
Box 669, Mankato, MN 56001

Contents

Introduction

What is a Race Car?

A race car is a beautiful machine. It has lots of chrome. The shape of the body is smooth. Air passes over it, around it and under it easily, without slowing it down.

On either side of a race car there is a racing number. Each car's colors and number help identify it.

Its fat racing tires are called "slicks." They are made of a special material that makes them hug the road.

Inside is an instrument panel. There is a **tachometer**. This tells the driver how fast his engine is running. The oil temperature and water temperature gauges tell him when the engine is running hot.

The race fans in the grandstands watch. The race cars go by so fast they look like a blur of bright colors. A race car is very powerful. It can go over 200 **m.p.h**.

A Brief History

Auto racing started when most people still used a horse and buggy to get around. That was back around 1900.

Grand Prix racing as we know it today came from the first French Grand Prix race. **Grand Prix** means "Great Prize" in French. The first Grand Prix was held in 1906 at the town of Le Mans in France.

The race cars were very large. They had big wheels and were very noisy. They raced on straight and curvy roads. They raced through towns and in the countryside.

As the sport of racing grew, a special race track needed to be built. This track needed to be safer for spectators and yet allow a good view of the track. The Indianapolis Speedway was built in Indianapolis, Indiana.

The first Indy 500 race was held in 1911. Ray Harroun was the first "500" winner and the first to drive without a mechanic. "You can't do that," one official argued. "It won't be safe. You need a man to watch out for cars coming up behind." That is when Ray Harroun had a great idea. He put a mirror in his car.

His race car, the Marmon Wasp, had a big number 32 painted on each side. Its body was shaped like a giant wasp. It had huge round wheels. It was the fastest car on the track. Its average speed was over 74 m.p.h.

At first Indy racing followed the Grand Prix race rules until 1930 when the Indianapolis officials decided to make their own rules. To this day they race by these rules.

The Indianapolis 500 is the best-attended auto sporting event in the United States. Each Memorial Day weekend over 400,000 fans come to the Indianapolis Speedway to cheer for their favorite driver. Millions of fans watch at home on their television.

A man named Bill France Sr. started the **National Association for Stock Car Racing** (NASCAR) in 1948. NASCAR helped give stock car racing its rules.

A new super speedway was built in 1950 called the Daytona International Speedway. The Daytona 500 race is held at this track located at

Daytona Beach, Florida. It is probably the most famous stock-car race in the world.

NASCAR started holding many races and called their races the Grand National series until the 1980s. Then the name was changed to Winston Cup. This was the name of the original sponsor for the races.

Types of Race Cars

GRAND PRIX (FORMULA 1)

The Grand Prix race rules are very strict. The race cars have to be built according to a certain formula. Formula 1 racing is the most danger-ous form of auto racing.

The Formula 1 car competes on the "Grand Prix, Formula 1 Circuit." The races lead to a world championship. The most famous Grand Prix, Formula 1 race is held on the streets of Monte Carlo, a town in Southern Europe.

Most of the Formula 1 cars race on a road

course. The road course has right- and left-hand turns. These turns are called **esses**. On a slower section you would have to slow down more for the curves. The races are held in any kind of weather.

INDY CARS

Indy cars that race in the Indianapolis 500 compete on an oval-shaped track. The track is known all over the world as the Brickyard. This dates back to when the race track was actually paved with bricks.

The Indy driver turns left at each corner as he travels around the track. He goes counterclockwise. There is a saying, "Always turn left!"

The garage area is called **Gasoline Alley**. This is where the mechanics work on the cars.

Familiar designs of Indy cars are Coyotes, Wildcats, Parnellis, Penskes and Eagles. The design of the cars are never exactly the same the following year.

STOCK CARS

Stock cars run on oval-shaped tracks like the Indy cars.

The stock cars are able to run the fastest on a track like the Daytona Speedway. Daytona is a high-banked track with steep corners. This bank helps the cars speed around without spinning out or crashing.

Stock cars can also be set up to run on road course like a Grand Prix (Formula 1) car. A famous road course that stock cars run on is at Watkins Glen in New York.

How Do Race Cars Differ From Regular Cars?

Indy cars and Formula 1 cars have one seat, an open cockpit, and open wheels. The wheels are not covered by fenders. These race cars have a low chassis. The driver sits very close to the ground. He drives in a position almost lying down. A race car can go over 200 m.p.h. on a straight stretch of road.

Race cars are built a special way to go very fast. Indy cars and Formula cars each have a body that looks like the fuselage of an airplane. Air passes over, around and under them easily without slowing them down.

To stop one of these race cars from skidding, there are small wings called "**airfoils**." As the air rushes over them, it pushes down on the car. This helps the wheels grip the road and go faster in turns.

The rules of Formula 1 are strict but there is plenty of room for technical experimenting. A Formula 1 race car may look like a low-slung bathtub on wheels. It can also have a wedge shape, or some odd feature which makes everyone stop and stare.

The steering on these race cars is like on a go cart. It is very small and very sensitive. It is easy to spin out.

Race car engines cost thousands of dollars. The engine of a Formula 1 or an Indy car is located behind the driver.

All kinds of engines have been experimented with in Formula 1 cars. Even gas turbine and rotary engines have been tried.

The turbo-charged engine on an Indy car or a Formula 1 car is very powerful. It makes use of its own exhaust to drive a special fan. The fan sucks extra air into the engine. This helps with

combustion and adds power.

There are turbo-charged cars on the regular market as well but they do not use the same fuel as an Indy Car or a Formula 1. These race car fuel mixtures contain alcohol or **nitromethane** instead of ordinary gasoline. This special fuel is like airplane fuel. It makes the race car go faster.

A stock car looks very much like your family car. But it has special modifications that make it go faster.

In the early days of racing "stock" really meant

"stock." It was the way a car came from the factory. Early stock cars even used street tires. The driver just added a roll bar to protect himself in case the car would roll over.

In the early 1950s the people in Detroit who were making cars started helping the big-name drivers in Winston Cup racing. They would provide the cars, parts, motors and technology. This has been true ever since.

Today a Winston Cup car still has to look like a car from the factory of the same year and make.

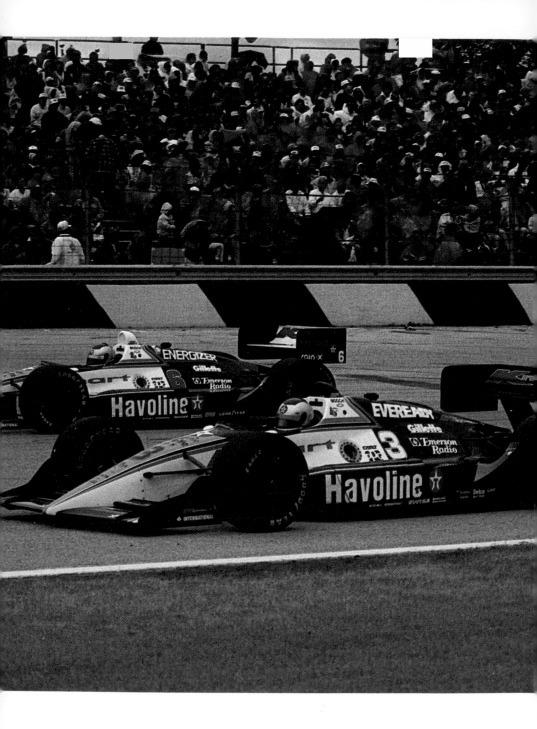

The body is generally made out of fiberglass instead of metal.

A Winston Cup stock car has to weigh 3700 pounds. These are the rules. This may seem to you like a lot of weight but under the shiny body is a welded tubular steel frame. It protects the driver on all sides. Heavy horizontal tubing protects the door area. A complete roll cage surrounds the driver. This is why when you see a car run into the wall, the driver often walks away with minor injuries.

In all race cars the **suspension** is a key factor in how well the car handles. The suspension is the way a car is connected to the axle and wheels. Special racing shock absorbers and springs are used in all racing suspension systems.

Good handling also depends on weight distribution. It takes good mechanics to know how to set up a race car so it will race very fast.

The Drivers

Mario Andretti is a world famous race car driver who has won Indy car races, stock car races and Grand Prix (Formula 1) races.

All Mario could think of when he was a young boy in Italy, was becoming a race car driver. After the war he moved with his family to the United States. He started racing stock cars first. He was not very good when he started, but he got better the more he tried.

Finally he started winning. When he won, he kept putting the money into a better car. He decided he wanted to race Indy cars.

At the Indy 500 in 1969, Mario had a brand-new car owned by Andy Granatelli, a race car

builder. It had a powerful Ford engine in a body built by the Lotus company of England. During practice the car went out of control and crashed into the wall. It was all smashed up.

Mario was strapped in the cockpit and burned when a fire broke out. But he was still determined to drive in the race. Since his new car was ruined, he had to race his older-model racer. It was a Brawner-Hawk Special. He had to qualify for his spot in the Indy race. The fastest car would get the best starting position for the race.

In qualifying, he was second-fastest of all the thirty-three contenders. Only one other top race car driver, A. J. Foyt, was faster. The Brawner-Hawk Special did so well in the race that Mario Andretti won the 1969 Indianapolis 500 race.

Other famous names in Indy racing today are Rick Mears, Emerson Fittipaldi, Danny Sullivan and Bobby Rahal. They are all Indianapolis 500 winners.

Mario Andretti also drove Formula 1s as did Emerson Fittipaldi. Other famous men who have driven Formula 1 racers are Sterling Moss, James Hunt, Alain Prost and Niki Lauda.

In stock car racing, some of the super heroes are Dale Earnhardt, Rusty Wallace, Bill Elliott, and Richard Petty.

Richard Petty's red and blue No. 43 is probably the most famous Winston Cup car of all. Petty is called the king of stock car racing because he has won the race for the checkered flag more than any other driver on record—200 times.

Richard's father, Lee, was a race car driver and

his son, Kyle, is also a race car driver. This is a three-generation racing family.

A race car driver is like a bullfighter in an arena. Everyone is watching to see if he will come out alive. Auto racing is a very dangerous sport.

Like other top athletes, you have to have great mental concentration. You have to be strong to drive a race car for 500 miles to win either the Daytona 500 or the Indy 500.

In all types of racing, the cars are all going very fast. A driver must have quick reflexes. It is important not to take your foot off the gas too fast or turn the wheel too sharply or you might spin out. You may go into the wall or hit a car. If you hit a car, that car may hit another car.

You need good vision to be a race car driver in order to judge distance. Braking, shifting gears and accelerating at high speeds take excellent coordination.

More than anything, you have to want to win.

Behind The Scenes

Indy racing, Formula 1 racing and stock car racing is more than just a sport. It is a business.

Besides the drivers, there are workers who keep the track clean. There are announcers, ticket sellers, and those who sell refreshments.

Before a race there is a technical inspection. The driver cannot enter a race until the technical inspector has given the final O.K. A check is made of all safety equipment. All cars must have seat belts, a fire extinguisher, and a roll bar. The roll bar is in case the race car overturns.

The driver wears a safety helmet and special clothing that is fire-resistant. He also wears a complete safety harness to stop him from being thrown from the car if it crashes.

If a driver should get seriously injured, he can get medical help at a mobile hospital at the race track.

During the race, a race car driver talks with his chief mechanic on a two-way radio. He tells him if he is having problems. There are only a few

seconds during pit stops to fix things.

The "**pit**" area is right alongside one section of the track. Each driver has his own pit space and his own crew. When the driver comes into the pits, each team member hurries to do what has to be done to get the car back on the track as fast as possible.

Tires may have to be changed. The car has to be fueled up. Generally, a limited number of

41

crew members are allowed over the pit wall during a pit stop. A crew member may pass a cold drink on the end of a pole to the driver.

A fast **pit crew** can make the difference of whether a team wins or loses.

In all types of racing there are rivalries among drivers. Each one wants to be the best.

For every race, you have to practice hard. Then you have to qualify for your position in the big race. Each lap of each car will be officially timed.

All kinds of things can go wrong in practice, in qualifying and when you are finally out there racing. A broken fuel line, overheated engine, or a blown tire can cost you the race.

The Future

Automobile racing is always changing and drivers are asking for better safety measures. In the future Indy cars and Formula 1 cars could be covered with a "Bubble" canopy. Tires may become wider, or oxygen will be provided through full-faced helmets so that vapor fumes are not breathed in.

Race car designers will certainly be trying out new materials. They will try out new types of engines and will look at new aerodynamic theories. Body shapes may change to some very far out designs.

In the future all race cars can use more microchip technology. The research has been going on for years but has yet to be fully developed.

45

Glossary

Airfoils: Small wings on race cars. The air rushes over them and help keep the wheels on the track so the car can go faster around curves.

Esses: Turns on a racing track.

Gasoline Alley: The garage area where mechanics work on Indy cars.

Grand Prix:: A famous race held in Le Mans, France. It means "Great Prize".

M.P.H.: Miles per hour, a measure of how fast a car can travel.

NASCAR: National Association for Stock Car Racing. It gives stock car racing its rules.

Nitromethane: A special fuel mixture with alcohol that is used in race cars.

Pit: The area at a race track where a driver can pull over for repairs and refueling during a race.

Pit Crew: A team of mechanics who work very fast in the pit. They can change tires, refuel and make minor repairs in a very short time.

Suspension: The way a car is attached to the axle and wheels. It is very important in the way a car handles on the road.

Tachometer: An instrument that tells a race car driver how fast his engine is running.